I Would Teach You to Fly

Sarah Asper-Smith

Illustrations by Mitchell Watley

little bigfoot
an imprint of sasquatch books
seattle, wa

For Neva Eileen — SAS & MW

Manufactured in China by C&C Offset Printing Co. Ltd.
Shenzhen, Guangdong Province, in June 2022

LITTLE BIGFOOT with colophon is a registered
trademark of Penguin Random House LLC

26 25 24 23 22   9 8 7 6 5 4 3 2 1

Editor: Christy Cox
Production editor: Jill Saginario
Book and cover designer: Alicia Terry

Library of Congress Cataloging-in-Publication Data
is available.

ISBN: 978-1-63217-404-8

Sasquatch Books
1325 Fourth Avenue, Suite 1025
Seattle, WA 98101

SasquatchBooks.com

FSC
www.fsc.org

MIX
Paper from
responsible sources
FSC® C008047

If you were a
bald eagle,

I would teach you to fly.

Juvenile (young) bald eagles appear larger than their parents.
They have longer wing feathers, which helps them learn to fly.

If you were a
black bear,

Black bears are excellent climbers, and cubs as young as six weeks old can climb trees.

I would teach you to pluck blueberries from a branch.

If you were a
gray whale,

I would teach you to make a journey of thousands of miles to the Arctic, where we would feast and fill our bellies.

Gray whales, unlike any other baleen whale, find food on the seafloor.

If you were an
ermine,

I would teach you to
tunnel through the snow.

An ermine's brown coat will change to white
during the winter months, but the tip of its tail
will stay black year-round.

If you were an
Arctic bumblebee,

I would teach you to fly from flower to flower, drinking nectar and collecting pollen.

Arctic bumblebee queens hibernate during the winter and wake to feed on willow trees' nectar when they start to blossom.

If you were a
great blue heron,

I would teach you to be still
and patient, and watch for fish.

Great blue herons spend almost all of
their waking life searching for food.

If you were a
spotted seal,

Spotted seal pups are born on
the ice, and don't enter the
water for several weeks.

I would teach you
to take deep, deep
dives underwater.

If you were a Sitka black-tailed deer,

A deer's ears move independently, so they can direct one ear to a sound without moving their heads.

I would teach you to
eat skunk cabbage,
a yellow sign of spring.

If you were a
Steller's jay,

I would teach you to imitate
other animals with your call
and make a sound like a cat or
a squirrel or another bird.

Steller's jays make nests in trees with twigs and pine needles and moss and mud.

If you were a
coyote,

Coyotes are great jumpers and can leap over thirteen feet horizontally.

I would teach you to hunt at night, walking on your tiptoes to be quiet.

If you were a
killer whale,

Killer whales travel, hunt, and live together
in groups called a pod.

I would teach you to sense the ocean world by whistling and clicking, making sounds that bounce off objects in your path.

If you were an **Arctic ground squirrel,**

Baby ground squirrels are born hairless, toothless, and blind.

I would teach you to dig your own burrow in our colony beneath the ground.

If you were a
willow ptarmigan,

I would teach you to roost
in a snowbank for a safe
place to sleep.

In the winter, ptarmigans grow feathers on their feet
to help them walk without sinking into the snow.

If you were a
Dall sheep,

I would teach you to climb
the steep cliffs and slopes
of the mountainside.

The curled horns of the male sheep will continue to grow every
year, and will eventually look like a circle from the side.

If you were
a **wolverine,**

I would teach you to be
fearless when on the
hunt for food.

A wolverine's sense of smell is excellent—they can detect prey twenty feet below the snow.

Because I love you,
I will teach you many
ways to live in this world.